W9-BOP-829

# The Silly Song-book

BY

## ESTHER L. NELSON

ILLUSTRATIONS BY JOYCE BEHR

Sterling Publishing Co., Inc.  New York
Distributed in the U.K. by Blandford Press

**Other Books of Interest**
Best Singing Games for Children of All Ages
Dancing Games for Children of All Ages
Holiday Singing and Dancing Games
Movement Games for Children of All Ages
Musical Games for Children of All Ages
Silly Verse (and Even Worse)
Singing and Dancing Games for the Very Young

**Acknowledgments**
Thanks to the Director, Staff and children
of the Mechanicsburg Learning Center,
Mechanicsburg, Pennsylvania, to Risa Sokolsky,
Jere Rosemeyer, Jill Tallmer, Abraham Levin,
Sylvia Kluth and to Hannah Reich for sharing
her wealth of songs with me. And
thanks to my great editor and friend Sheila
Barry, for making it possible once more.

# CONTENTS

To the loving memory of my marvelous,
musical mother . . . . . . . . . .Freda Nelson

# CRAZY CHARACTERS

# Boom Boom, Ain't It Great to be Crazy?

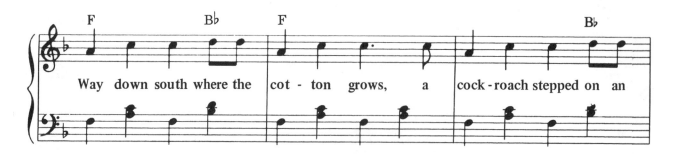

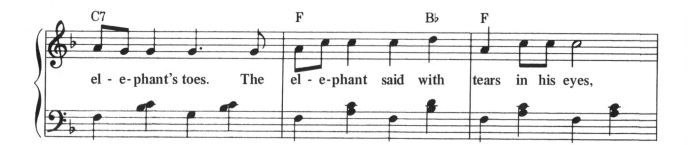

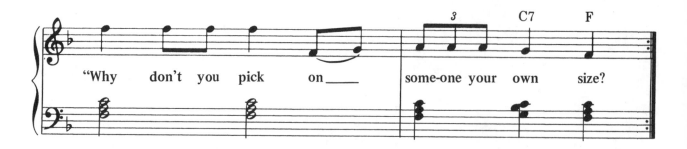

Way down south where the cotton grows,
A cockroach stepped on an elephant's toes.
The elephant said, with tears in his eyes,
"Why don't you pick on someone your
        own size?"

**Chorus**
Boom boom, ain't it great to be cra-zy?
Boom boom, ain't it great to be nuts?
Giddy and foolish all the day long,
Boom boom, ain't it great to be cra-zy!

# Boom Boom, Ain't It Great to be Crazy?

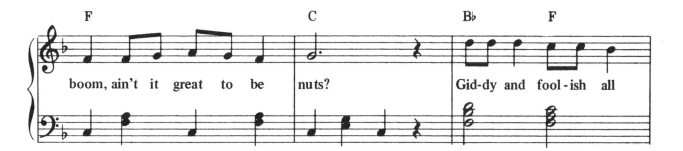

From *Dancing Games for Children of All Ages*
© 1973 by Esther L. Nelson, reprinted by permission of Sterling Publishing Co., Inc.

I bought a suit of combination underwear,
Can't get if off, I do declare.
Wore it six months without exaggeration.
Can't get it off, 'cause I lost the
    combination.

**Chorus**

Fuzzy Wuzzy was a bear,
And Fuzzy Wuzzy cut his hair,
So Fuzzy Wuzzy wasn't fuzzy.
No, by Jove, he wasn't, wuz he?

**Chorus**

A horse and a flea and three blind mice
Sat on a tombstone, eating rice.
The horse he slipped and fell on the flea.
"Whoops," said the flea, "there's a horse
    on me!"

**Chorus**

Up in the north and a long way off,
A donkey got the whooping cough.
He coughed so hard, his head fell off—
Up in the north and a long way off.

**Chorus**

# Boom Boom, Ain't It Great to be Crazy? (continued)

I love myself—I think I'm grand.
When I go to the movies I hold my hand.
I put my arm around my waist,
And when I get fresh, I slap my face.

**Chorus**

I call myself on the telephone.
Just to hear my musical tone.
I ask myself for a heavy date.
And I pick myself up at half-past eight.

**Chorus**

I take a swim in my swimming pool.
I jump from the board, 'cause that's the
    rule.
I hit my head on cement and mortar.
Forgot to look—there was no water!

**Chorus**

Way up north where there's ice and snow,
There lived a penguin, name of Joe.
He got so tired of black and white,
He wore technicolor pants to the dance last
    night.

**Chorus**

That one-eared cat, who used to sit
Watching grandma rock and knit,
Swallowed a ball of bright red yarn—
And out came her kittens with red
    sweaters on.

**Chorus**

# Johnny's Lost His Marble

From *The Funny Family* © 1978 by Alison McMorland, reprinted by permission of Ward Lock Educational.

# Johnny's Lost His Marble

Johnny's lost his marble,
Johnny's lost his marble,
Johnny's lost his marble
Down in Granny's yard.

He lost it up the drainpipe,
He lost it up the drainpipe,
He lost it up the drainpipe
Down in Granny's yard.

He went and got the clothes prop,
He went and got the clothes prop,
He went and got the clothes prop
Down in Granny's yard.

He rammed it up the drainpipe,
He rammed it up the drainpipe,
He rammed it up the drainpipe
Down in Granny's yard.

Still he didn't find it,
Still he didn't find it,
Still he didn't find it
Down in Granny's yard.

So he went and got a broomstick,
He went and got a broomstick,
He went and got a broomstick
Down in Granny's yard.

He tied it to the clothes prop,
He tied it to the clothes prop,
He tied it to the clothes prop
Down in Granny's yard.

And he rammed it up the drainpipe,
He rammed it up the drainpipe,
He rammed it up the drainpipe
Down in Granny's yard.

Still he couldn't find it,
Still he couldn't find it,
Still he couldn't find it
Down in Granny's yard.

He went for the policeman,
He went for the policeman,
He went for the policeman
Down in Granny's yard.

And he tied him to the clothes prop,
He tied him to the clothes prop,
He tied him to the clothes prop
Down in Granny's yard.

He rammed him up the drainpipe,
He rammed him up the drainpipe,
He rammed him up the drainpipe
Down in Granny's yard.

Still he couldn't find it,
Still he couldn't find it,
Still he couldn't find it
Down in Granny's yard.

So he went and got gunpowder,
He went and got gunpowder,
He went and got gunpowder
Down in Granny's yard.

He tied it to the clothes prop,
He tied it to the clothes prop,
He tied it to the clothes prop
Down in Granny's yard.

He rammed it up the drainpipe,
He rammed it up the drainpipe,
He rammed it up the drainpipe
And *blew up* Granny's yard.

Johnny found his marble,
Johnny found his marble,
Johnny found his marble
Down in Granny's yard.

Twas in his blooming pocket,
Twas in his blooming pocket,
Twas in his blooming pocket
DOWN IN GRANNY'S YARD!

# Dear Old Daddy's Whiskers

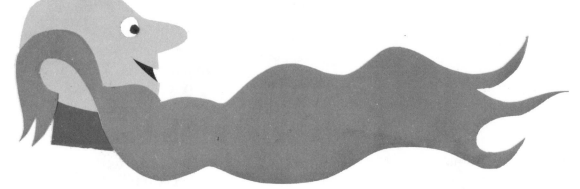

We have a dear old Daddy
Whose hair is silver gray.
He has a set of whiskers—
They're always in the way.

**Chorus**
Oh, they're always in the way.
The cow eats them for hay.
Mother eats them in her sleep,
She thinks she's eating shredded wheat,
They're always in the way.

We have a dear old Mommy,
She likes his whiskers, too.
She uses them for cleaning
And stirring up a stew.

**Chorus**

We have a dear old brother,
Who has a Ford machine.
He uses Daddy's whiskers
To strain the gasoline.

**Chorus**

We have a dear old sister.
It really is a laugh.
She sprinkles Daddy's whiskers
As bath salts in her bath.

**Chorus**

We have another sister,
Her name is Ida Mae.
She climbs up Daddy's whiskers
And braids them every day.

**Chorus**

Around the supper table,
We make a merry group,
Until dear Daddy's whiskers
Get tangled in the soup.

**Chorus**

Daddy was in battle,
He wasn't killed, you see:
His whiskers looked like bushes,
And fooled the enemy.

**Chorus**

When Daddy goes in swimming,
No bathing suit for him.
He ties his whiskers 'round his waist,
And happily jumps in.

**Chorus**

# Dear Old Daddy's Whiskers

We have a dear old Dad-dy, whose hair is sil-ver

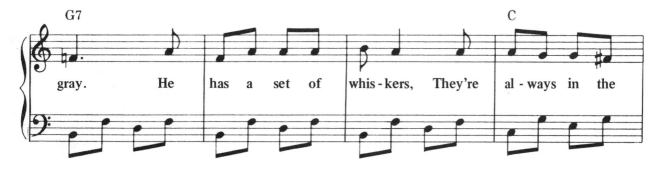

gray. He has a set of whis-kers, They're al-ways in the

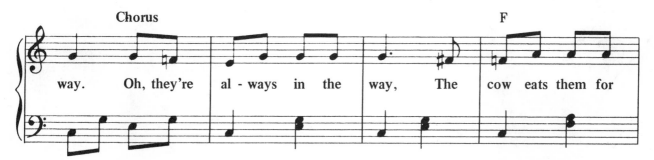

**Chorus**

way. Oh, they're al-ways in the way, The cow eats them for

hay. Moth-er eats them in her sleep, She thinks she's eat-ing

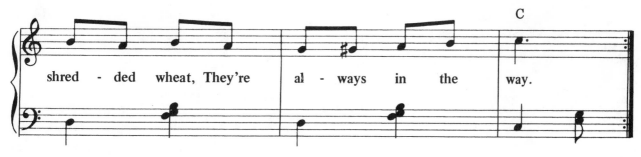

shred-ded wheat, They're al-ways in the way.

# Jenny Jenkins

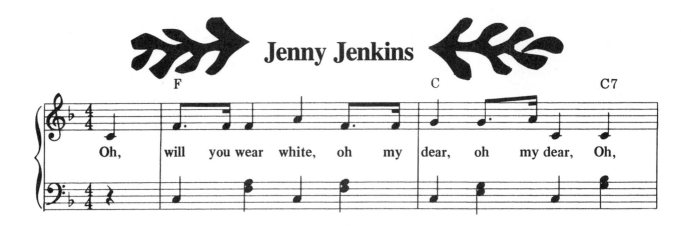

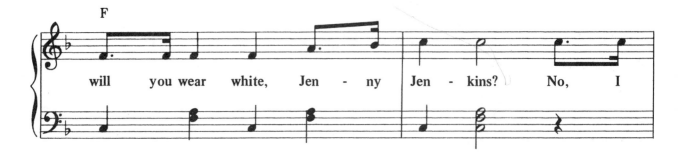

will you wear white, Jen - ny Jen - kins? No, I

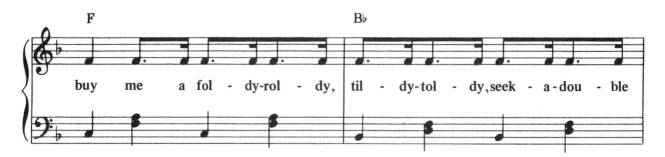

won't wear white, 'cause the col - or is too bright, And I'll

buy me a fol - dy-rol - dy, til - dy-tol - dy, seek - a-dou - ble

use - a-cause - a roll to find me Roll, Jen - ny Jen - kins, roll.

 # Jenny Jenkins

Oh, will you wear white, oh my dear, oh
my dear,
Oh, will you wear white, Jenny Jenkins?
No, I won't wear white—'cause the color
is too bright—

**Chorus**

And I'll buy me a foldy-roldy, tildy-toldy,
Seek-a-double use-a-cause-a roll to find
me—
Roll, Jenny Jenkins, roll.

Oh, will you wear red, oh my dear, oh my
dear,
Oh, will you wear red, Jenny Jenkins?
No, I won't wear red—it's the color of my
head—

**Chorus**

Oh, will you wear yellow, oh my dear, oh
my dear,
Oh, will you wear yellow, Jenny Jenkins?
No, I won't wear yellow, when I go out
with my fellow—

**Chorus**

Oh, will you wear green, oh my dear, oh
my dear,
Oh, will you wear green, Jenny Jenkins?
No, I won't wear green—like a limp
string bean—

**Chorus**

Oh, will you wear brown, oh my dear, oh
my dear,
Oh, will you wear brown, Jenny Jenkins?
No, I won't wear brown—that's no color
for a gown—

**Chorus**

Oh, will you wear gold, oh my dear, oh my
dear,
Oh, will you wear gold, Jenny Jenkins?
No, I won't wear gold—I'd look too old—

**Chorus**

Oh, will you wear rose, oh my dear, oh my
dear,
Oh, will you wear rose, Jenny Jenkins?
No, I won't wear rose—it's the color of my
nose—

**Chorus**

Oh, will you wear cotton, oh my dear, oh
my dear,
Oh, will you wear cotton, Jenny Jenkins?
No, I won't wear cotton, 'cause cotton
feels rotten—

**Chorus**

Oh, will you wear a coat, oh my dear, oh
my dear,
Oh, will you wear a coat, Jenny Jenkins?
No, I won't wear a coat, like any old goat.

**Chorus**

Oh, will you wear shoes, oh my dear, oh
my dear,
Oh, will you wear shoes, Jenny Jenkins?
No, I won't wear shoes—and that's good
news!

**Chorus**

Oh, what will you wear, oh my dear, oh my
dear,
Oh, what will you wear, Jenny Jenkins?
Oh, I really don't care if I go bare—

**Chorus**

# Miss Lucy Had a Baby

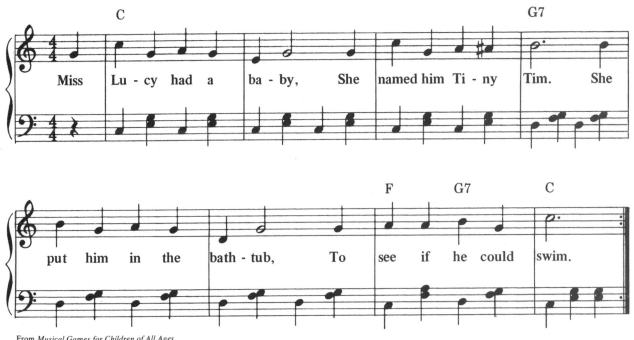

Miss Lu-cy had a ba-by, She named him Ti-ny Tim. She
put him in the bath-tub, To see if he could swim.

From *Musical Games for Children of All Ages*
© 1976 by Esther L. Nelson, reprinted by permission of Sterling Publishing Co., Inc.

Miss Lucy had a baby.
She named him Tiny Tim.
She put him in the bathtub
To see if he could swim.

He drank up all the water,
He ate up all the soap,
He tried to eat the bathtub
But it wouldn't go down his throat.

He floated up the river.
He floated down the lake.
And now Miss Lucy's baby
Has got a bellyache.

Miss Lucy called the Doctor,
Miss Lucy called the Nurse,
Miss Lucy called the lady
With the alligator purse.

"Measles," said the Doctor,
"Mumps," said the Nurse,
"A virus," said the lady
With the alligator purse.

"Penicillin," said the Doctor,
"Bed rest," said the Nurse,
"Pizza," said the lady
With the alligator purse.

"He'll live," said the Doctor,
"He's all right," said the Nurse,
"I'm leaving," said the lady
With the alligator purse.

Miss Lucy gave me peaches,
And then she gave me pears,
And then she gave me fifty cents
And kicked me up the stairs.

My mother was born in England,
My father was born in France,
And I was born in diapers
Because I had no pants.

14

# There Was a Man and He Was Mad

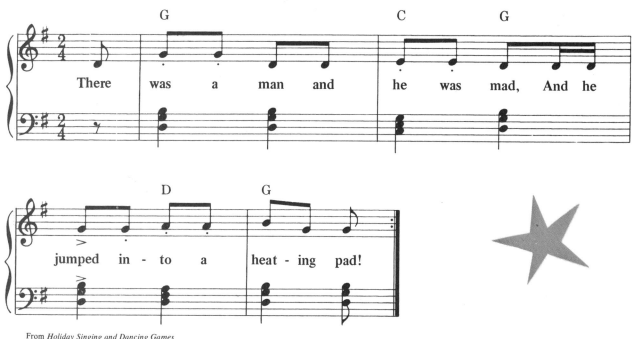

From *Holiday Singing and Dancing Games*

There was a man and he was mad,
And he *jumped* into a heating pad!

The heating pad it got so hot
That he *jumped* into a honey pot!

The honey pot it was so dark
That he *jumped* into a doggie bark!

The doggie's bark it was so loud
That he *jumped* into a big white cloud!

The big white cloud it was so high
That he *jumped* way up to the top of the
  sky!

Another man was just as mad,
And he *jumped* into a shopping bag.

The paper bag it was so narrow
That he *jumped* into a wheelbarrow.

The wheelbarrow ran away
And *bumped* into a cart of hay.

The cart of hay it caught on fire
And flew him up to Jeremiah.

Jeremiah was full of stones
And so they broke the mad man's bones.

# Oh, How He Lied!

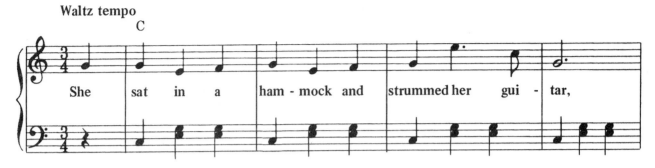

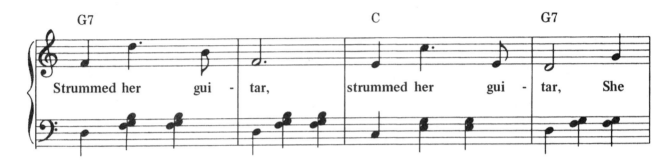

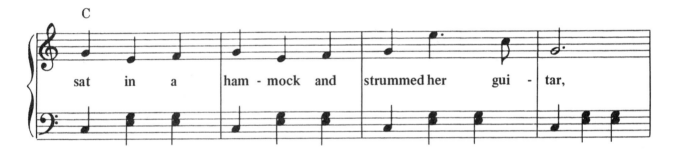

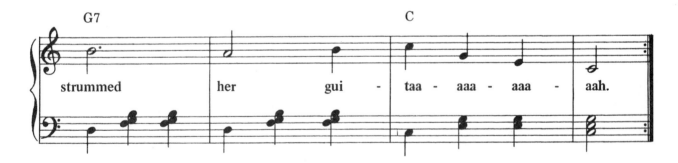

# Oh, How He Lied!

She sat in a hammock and strummed her
    guitar,
Strummed her guitar, strummed her guitar.
She sat in a hammock and strummed her
    guitar,
Strummed  her gui-taa--aaa--aaa--aah.

He sat down beside her and smoked a
    cigar,
Smoked a cigar, smoked a cigar.
He sat down beside her and smoked a
    cigar,
Smoked a ci--gaa--aaa--aaa--aah.

He told her he loved her, but oh how he
    lied!
Oh, how he lied, oh, how he lied!
He told her he loved her, but oh how he
    lied!
Oh, how he lie--ie--iee--ied.

She told him she loved him, and oh how
    she sighed!
Oh, how she sighed, oh, how she sighed!
She told him she loved him, but oh how she
    sighed!
Oh, how she sigh--igh--igh--ighed.

Now she got pneumonia, and she ups and
    died,
She upups and died, she uups and died.
Now she got pneumonia, and she uups and
    died.
She uups and die--ie--ie--ied.

He went to the funeral just for the ride,
Just for the ride, just for the ride.
He went to the funeral just for the ride,
Just for the ri--ii---ii---ide.

He sat on her tombstone and "Boo hoo,"
    he cried.
"Boo hoo," he cried. "Boo hoo," he cried.
He sat on her tombstone and "Boo hoo,"
    he cried,
"Boo hoo," he cri--ie--ie--ied.

Now she went to heaven and flip flap she
    flied,
Flip flap, she flied, flip flap, she flied.
Now she went to heaven and flip flap, she
    flied.
Flip, flap, she fli--ie--ie--ed.

Now he went to mmmm
            and sizzled and fried,
Sizzled and fried, sizzled and fried
Now he went to mmmm
            and sizzled and fried,
Sizzled  and fri--ie--ie--ied.

The moral of the story is don't tell a lie,
Don't tell a lie, don't tell a lie.
The moral of the story is don't tell a lie,
Don't tell a lie--ie--ie--ie.

# I'm a Nut

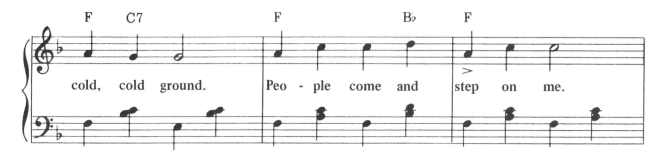

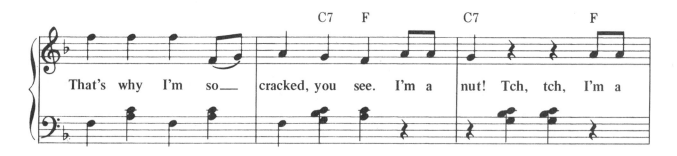

From *Holiday Singing and Dancing Games*
© 1980 by Esther L. Nelson, reprinted by permission of Sterling Publishing Co., Inc.

I'm a little acorn, small and round,
Lying on the cold, cold ground.
People come and step on me.
That's why I'm so cracked, you see.

**Chorus**

I'm a nut! Tch, tch,
I'm a nut! Tch, tch,
I'm a nut! Tch, tch,
I'm a nut! Tch, tch.

# ODD ✦ AND EVEN ✦ ANIMALS

# Mr. Frog Went A-Courtin'

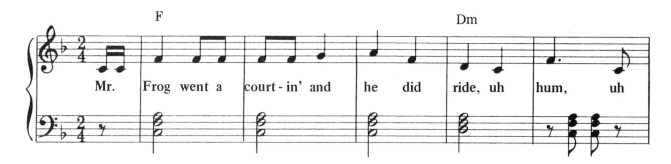

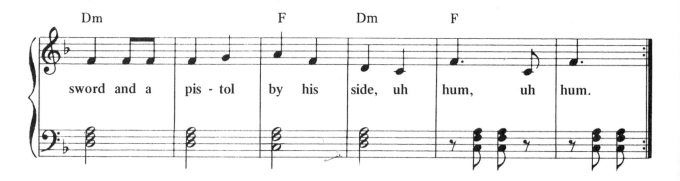

Mr. Frog went a-courtin' and he did ride,
    uh hum, uh hum,
Mr. Frog went a-courtin' and he did ride,
A sword and a pistol by his side,
    uh hum, uh hum.

He rode up to Miss Mousie's den,
    uh hum, uh hum,
He rode up to Miss Mousie's den,
And he said, "Miss Mousie, are you
    within?" uh hum, uh hum.

"Oh yes sir, here I sit and spin,"
    uh hum, uh hum,
"Oh yes sir, here I sit and spin,
Just lift the latch and please come in,"
    uh hum, uh hum.

He took Miss Mousie on his knee,
    uh hum, uh hum,
He took Miss Mousie on his knee,
And he said, "Miss Mousie, will you marry
    me?" uh hum, uh hum.

# Mr. Frog Went A-Courtin'

"I'll have to ask my Uncle Rat,"
      uh hum, uh hum,
"I'll have to ask my Uncle Rat
To see what he will say to that,"
      uh hum, uh hum.

"Without my Uncle Rat's consent,"
      uh hum, uh hum,
"Without my Uncle Rat's consent,
I wouldn't even marry the President,"
      uh hum, uh hum.

Now Uncle Rat when he came home,
      uh hum, uh hum,
Now Uncle Rat when he came home said,
"Who's been here since I've been gone?"
      uh hum, uh hum.

"A very fine gentleman has been here,"
      uh hum, uh hum,
"A very fine gentleman has been here
Who wishes to make me his dear,"
      uh hum, uh hum.

So Uncle Rat gave his consent,
      uh hum, uh hum,
So Uncle Rat gave his consent,
And made a handsome settlement,
      uh hum, uh hum.

Then Uncle Rat he went to town,
      uh hum, uh hum,
Then Uncle Rat he went to town
To buy his niece a wedding gown,
      uh hum, uh hum.

The first to the wedding was a flying moth,
      uh hum, uh hum,
The first to the wedding was a flying moth,
And she laid out the tablecloth,
      uh hum, uh hum.

The next to the wedding was the Juney
      bug, uh hum, uh hum,
The next to the wedding was the Juney
bug,
Carrying the water jug,
      uh hum, uh hum.

The next to the wedding was Old Raccoon,
      uh hum, uh hum,
The next to the wedding was Old Raccoon,
Eating with a silver spoon,
      uh hum, uh hum.

The next to the wedding was Mrs. Cow,
      uh hum, uh hum,
The next to the wedding was Mrs. Cow.
She tried to dance but she didn't know
      how, uh hum, uh hum.

The next to the wedding was Mr. Mole,
      uh hum, uh hum,
The next to the wedding was Mr. Mole.
He fell into a gopher hole,
      uh hum, uh hum.

# Mr. Frog Went A-Courtin' (continued)

The next to the wedding was a Big Tom
    Cat, uh hum, uh hum,
The next to the wedding was a Big Tom
    Cat.
He chased Miss Mousie and Uncle Rat,
    uh hum, uh hum.

The next to the wedding was a bumblebee,
    uh hum, uh hum,
The next to the wedding was a bumblebee,
A fiddle buckled on his knee,
    uh hum, uh hum.

The next to the wedding was the Old Gray
    Goose, uh hum, uh hum,
The next to the wedding was the Old Gray
    Goose.
She picked up a fiddle and really cut loose,
    uh hum, uh hum.

And what do you think they had for a
    fiddle, uh hum, uh hum,
And what do you think they had for a
    fiddle?
An old banjo with a hole in the middle,
    uh hum, uh hum.

And what do you think they had for supper,
    uh hum, uh hum,
And what do you think they had for
    supper?
A fried mosquito without any butter,
    uh hum, uh hum.

And what do you think they had to drink,
    uh hum, uh hum,
And what do you think they had to drink?
Cole slaw juice and a bottle of ink,
    uh hum, uh hum.

The next to the wedding was the spotted
    snake, uh hum, uh hum,
The next to the wedding was the spotted
    snake,
Passing out the wedding cake,
    uh hum, uh hum.

They all went rowing on the lake,
    uh hum, uh hum,
They all went rowing on the lake,
But they all got swallowed by a big black
    snake, uh hum, uh hum.

So that's the end of one, two, three,
    uh hum, uh hum,
So that's the end of one, two, three,
The Frog, the Rat and Miss Mousie,
    uh hum, uh hum.

There's bread and cheese upon the shelf,
    uh hum, uh hum,
There's bread and cheese upon the shelf.
If you want any more, just help yourself,
    uh hum, uh hum.

# My Father Hunted a Kangaroo

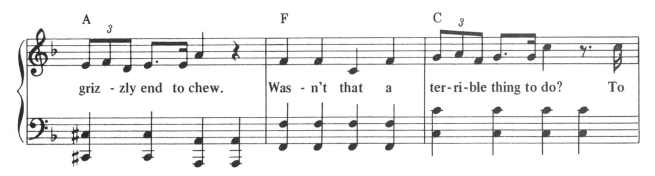

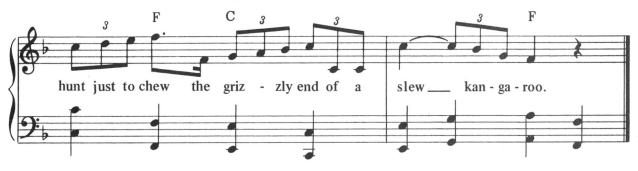

My father hunted a kangaroo,
Just for a grizzly end to chew.
Wasn't that a terrible thing to do?
To hunt just to chew the grizzly end of a slew kangaroo.

# Oh, I Had a Silly ~~Chicken~~ TURKEY

Oh, I had a sil - ly chick - en And he

would - n't lay an egg, So I poured hot wa - ter Up and

down his leg, And he gig - gled and he gig - gled And he

gig - gled all the day, And my poor lit - tle chick - en laid a

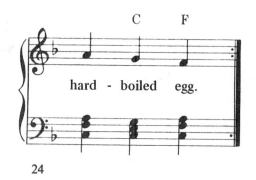

hard - boiled egg.

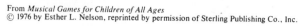

# Oh, I Had a Silly ~~Chicken~~ Turkey

Oh, I had a silly chicken
And he wouldn't lay an egg,
So I poured hot water
Up and down his leg,
And he giggled and he giggled,
And he giggled all the day,
And my poor little chicken
Laid a hard-boiled egg!

Oh, I had a silly chicken
And he wouldn't lay an egg,
So I poured hot water
Up and down his leg,
And he sang a silly song
Which turned out to be a ballad,
And my chicken laid a sandwich
Filled with egg and tuna (tune o') salad.

Oh, I had a silly chicken
He went scratching in the dirt,
And he scratched so hard
That his feet—they hurt.
So he bandaged them way up
From the thigh bone to his toe.
And you should have seen that chicken
Do a do-si-do!

# Old Hogan's Goat

There was a man
    (there was a man),
Now please take note
    (now please take note),
There was a man
    (there was a man)
Who had a goat
    (who had a goat).
He loved that goat
    (he loved that goat),
Indeed he did
    (indeed he did).
He loved that goat
    (he loved that goat),
Just like a kid
    (just like a kid)!

One day that goat
    (one day that goat)
Was feeling fine—
    (was feeling fine—)
Ate three red shirts
    (ate three red shirts)
Right off the line.
    (right off the line).
His master came
    (his master came)
And beat his back
    (and beat his back)
And tied him to
    (and tied him to)
A railroad track.
    (a railroad track).

The whistle blew
    (too, too, too, too).
The train drew nigh.
    (the train drew nigh)
The poor goat knew
    (the poor goat knew)
That he must die.
    (that he must die).
He gave three shrieks
    (eek, eek, eek, eek)
Of mortal pain,
    (of mortal pain)
Coughed up the shirts
    (coughed up the shirts)
And flagged the train!
    (and flagged the train).

# Old Hogan's Goat

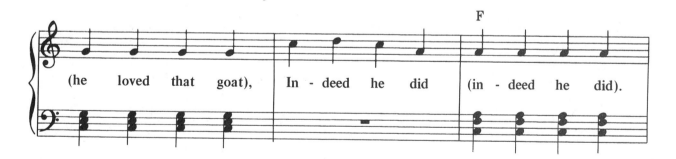

# Turkey in the Straw

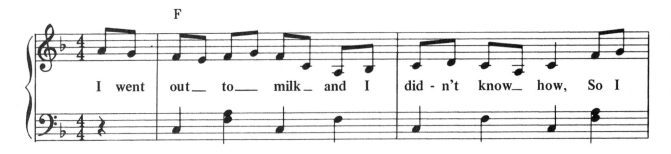

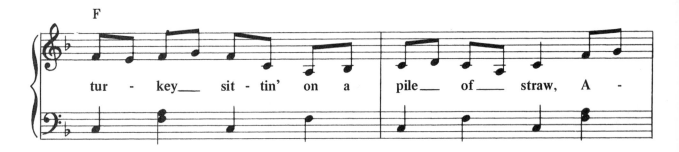

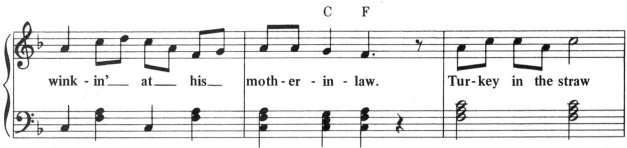

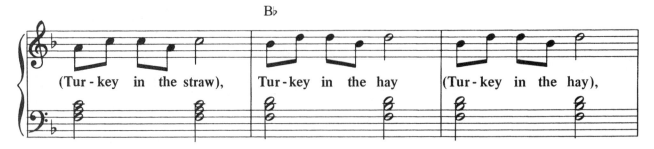

# Turkey in the Straw

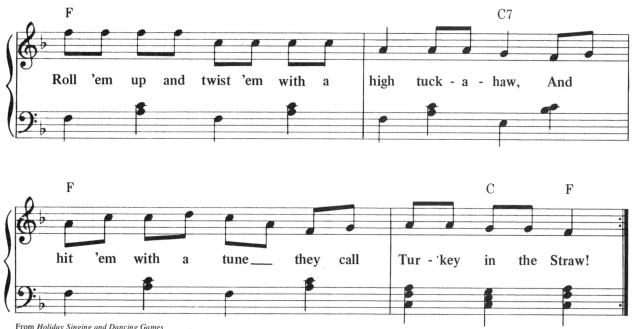

Roll 'em up and twist 'em with a high tuck - a - haw, And hit 'em with a tune___ they call Tur - key in the Straw!

I went out to milk and I didn't know how,
So I milked the goat instead of the cow.
Saw a turkey sittin' on a pile of straw,
A-winkin' at his mother-in-law.

### Chorus
Turkey in the straw (turkey in the straw),
Turkey in the hay (turkey in the hay),
Roll 'em up and twist 'em with a high
    tuck-a-haw,
And hit 'em with a tune they call "Turkey
    in the Straw!"

### Chorus

I met an old catfish, swimmin' in the
    stream.
I asked that old catfish, "What do you
    mean?"
I grabbed that catfish right by the snout,
And turned Mister Catfish wrongside out!

### Chorus

# Turkey in the Straw (continued)

I love to go a-fishin' on a bright summer
     day,
To see the perches and the catfish play,
With their hands in their pockets and their
     pockets in their pants.
Oh, I love to see the fishes do the
     hootchie-kootchie dance!

**Chorus**

Well, if frogs had wings and snakes had hair
And automobiles went a-flying through the
     air—
Well, if watermelons grew on the
     huckleberry vine,
We'd all have winter in the summertime.

**Chorus**

Oh, I went to Toledo and I walked around
     the block,
And I walked right into the baker's shop.
And I took two doughnuts out of the
     grease,
And I handed the lady there a five-cent
     piece.

**Chorus**

Oh, she looked at the nickel, and she
     looked at me,
And she said, "This money is no good, you
     see.
There's a hole in the middle and it goes
     right through."
Says I, "There's a hole in the doughnut,
     too!"

**Chorus**

● ● ● ● ● ● ● ● ● ● ● ● ● ●

# F e Little Monkeys

Five little monkeys jumping on the bed,
One fell off and bumped his head.
Mama called the Doctor and the Doctor
     said,
"No more monkey business jumping on the
     bed!"

Four little monkeys jumping on the bed,
One fell off and bumped his head.
Mama called the Doctor and the Doctor
     said,
"No more monkey business jumping on the
     bed!"

# Five Little Monkeys

Three little monkeys jumping on the bed,
One fell off and bumped his head.
Mama called the Doctor and the Doctor said,
"No more monkey business jumping on the bed!"

Two little monkeys jumping on the bed,
One fell off and bumped his head.
Mama called the Doctor and the Doctor said,
"No more monkey business jumping on the bed!"

One little monkey jumping on the bed,
He fell off and bumped his head.
Mama called the Doctor and the Doctor said,
"No more monkey business jumping on the bed!"

No more monkeys jumping on the bed.
No more monkeys bumping their head.
No more calling Doctors, and Doctors no more said,
"No more monkey business jumping on the bed!"

# Be Kind to Your Web-footed Friends

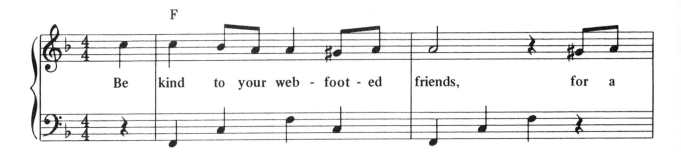

Be kind to your web - foot - ed friends, for a

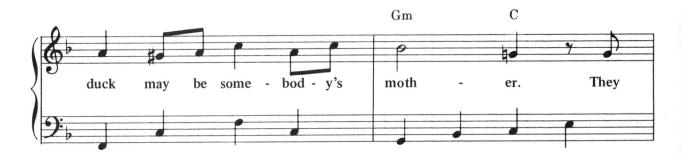

duck may be some - bod - y's moth - er. They

live in the bot-tom of the swamp, where the wea - ther is cold and

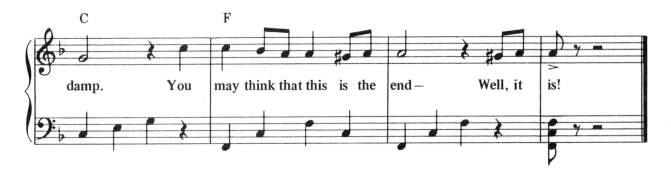

damp. You may think that this is the end— Well, it is!

Be kind to your web-footed friends,
For a duck may be somebody's mother.
They live in the bottom of the swamp,
Where the weather is cold and damp
     (d-ah-mp).
You may think that this is the end—
Well, it is!

# MAKE UP
# YOUR OWN
# VERSES

# A-Hunting We Will Go

From *Singing and Dancing Games for the Very Young*
© 1978 by Esther L. Nelson, reprinted by permission of Sterling Publishing Co., Inc.

Oh, a-hunting we will go,
A-hunting we will go,
We'll catch a fox
And put him in a box,
And then we'll let him go.

Oh, a-hunting we will go,
A-hunting we will go,
We'll catch a bear
And wash his hair,
And then we'll let him go.

Oh, a-hunting we will go,
A-hunting we will go,
We'll catch a snake
And give him a shake,
And then we'll let him go.

Oh, a-hunting we will go,
A-hunting we will go,
We'll catch a goose
By her caboose
And then we'll let her go.

# A-Hunting We Will Go

Oh, a-hunting we will go,
A-hunting we will go,
We'll catch a horse
And ride him, of course,
And then we'll let him go.

Oh, a-hunting we will go,
A-hunting we will go,
We'll catch a pig
And dance him a jig,
And then we'll let him go.

Oh, a-hunting we will go,
A-hunting we will go,
We'll catch a brontosaurus
And put him in the chorus,
And then we'll let him go.

Oh, a-hunting we will go,
A-hunting we will go,
We'll catch a crocodile
And we'll teach him how to smile
And then we'll let him go.

Oh, a-hunting we will go,
A-hunting we will go,
We'll catch a chicken
And give her a lickin'
And then we'll let her go.

Oh, a-hunting we will go,
A-hunting we will go,
We'll catch a dinosaur
In the dresser drawer
And then we'll let him go.

Oh, a-hunting we will go,
A-hunting we will go,
We'll catch a mouse
And we'll all play house
And then we'll let him go.

Oh, a-hunting we will go,
A-hunting we will go,
We'll catch a spider
And then we'll hide her
And then we'll let her go.

Oh, a-hunting we will go,
A-hunting we will go,
We'll catch a meanie
In a pink bikini
And then we'll let her go.

Oh, a-hunting we will go,
A-hunting we will go,
We'll catch a fly
And make him cry
And then we'll let him go.

# Aiken Drum

There was a man lived in the moon,
Lived in the moon, lived in the moon.
There was a man lived in the moon,
And his name was Aiken Drum.

**Chorus**
And he played upon a ladle,
       a ladle, a ladle,
And he played upon a ladle,
And his name was Aiken Drum.

And his hat was made of pudding,
      of pudding, of pudding,
And his hat was made of pudding,
And his name was Aiken Drum.

**Chorus**

And his coat was made of turkey,
      of turkey, of turkey,
And his coat was made of turkey,
And his name was Aiken Drum.

**Chorus**

And his belt was made of licorice,
      of licorice, of licorice,
And his belt was made of licorice,
And his name was Aiken Drum.

**Chorus**

And his pants were made of fish sticks,
     of fish sticks, of fish sticks,
And his pants were made of fish sticks
And his name was Aiken Drum.

**Chorus**

And his buttons were made of walnuts,
     of walnuts, of walnuts,
And his buttons were made of walnuts,
And his name was Aiken Drum.

**Chorus**

And his hair was made of spaghetti,
     of spaghetti, of spaghetti,
And his hair was made of spaghetti,
And his name was Aiken Drum.

**Chorus**

And his eyes were made of jelly beans,
     of jelly beans, of jelly beans,
And his eyes were made of jelly beans,
And his name was Aiken Drum.

**Chorus**

And his mouth was made of marshmallow,
     of marshmallow, of marshmallow,
And his mouth was made of marshmallow,
And his name was Aiken Drum.

**Chorus**

And his nose was made of nose drops,
     of nose drops, of nose drops,
And his nose was made of nose drops,
And his name was Aiken Drum.

**Chorus**

# Aiken Drum

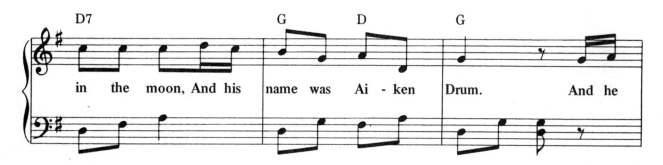

# You Can't Get to Heaven

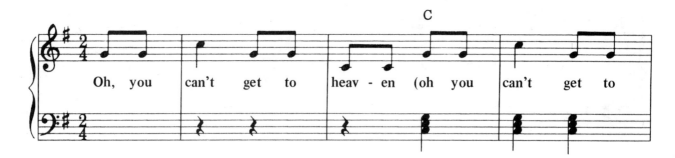

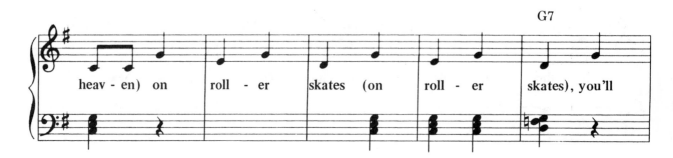

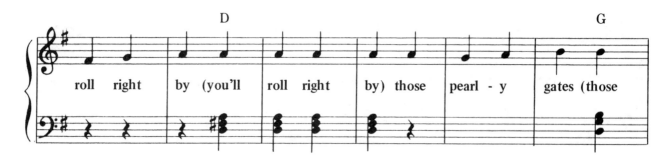

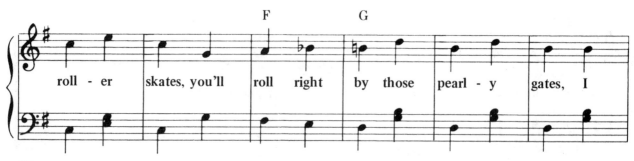

# You Can't Get to Heaven

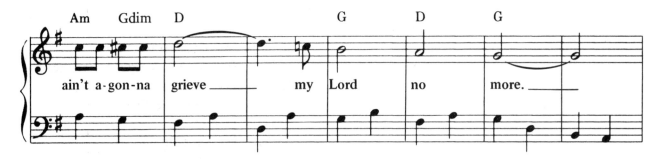

ain't a-gon-na grieve _____ my Lord no more. _____

Chorus

I ain't a-gon-na grieve my Lord no more, I

ain't a-gon-na grieve my Lord no more, I ain't a-gon-na

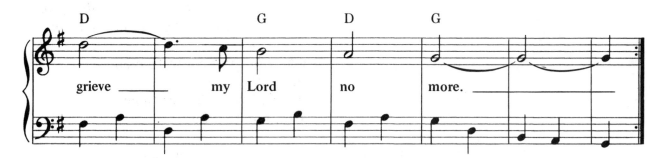

grieve _____ my Lord no more. _____

# You Can't Get to Heaven (continued)

Oh, you can't get to heaven
    (oh, you can't get to heaven)
On roller skates
    (on roller skates)
You'll roll right by
    (you'll roll right by)
Those pearly gates
    (those pearly gates)

**Chorus**
Oh, you can't get to heaven
On roller skates—
You'll roll right by
Those pearly gates—
I ain't a-gonna grieve
My Lord no more.
I ain't a-gonna grieve my Lord no more,
I ain't a-gonna grieve my Lord no more,
I ain't a-gonna grieve my Lord no more.

Oh, you can't get to heaven
In a rocking chair.
'Cause the rocking chair
Won't take you there.

**Chorus**
(*substitute each new thing that
"you can't get to heaven" in*)

Oh, you can't get to heaven
In a trolley car,
'Cause the gosh darn thing
Won't go that far.

**Chorus***

Oh, you can't get to heaven
On a rocket ship,
'Cause a rocket ship
Won't make the trip.

**Chorus***

# You Can't Get to Heaven (continued)

Oh, you can't get to heaven,
On a pair of skis,
'Cause you'll schuss right through
St. Peter's knees.

**Chorus**\*

Oh, you can't get to heaven,
In a limousine,
'Cause the Lord don't sell
No gasoline.

**Chorus**\*

Oh, you can't get to heaven
With powder and paint,
'Cause the Lord don't want
You as you ain't.

**Chorus**\*

Oh, you can't get to heaven
With Superman,
'Cause the Lord he is
A Batman fan.

**Chorus**\*

You can't chew tobaccy
On that golden shore,
'Cause the Lord don't have
No cuspidor.

**Chorus**\*

Oh, the devil is mad
And I am glad,
He lost a soul,
He thought he had.

**Chorus**\*

# You Can't Get to Heaven (continued)

If you get to heaven
Before I do,
Just bore a hole
And pull me through.

**Chorus**\*

If I get to heaven
Before you do,
I'll plug that hole
With shavings and glue!

**Chorus**\*

''That's all there is—
There ain't no more,''
St. Peter said,
And closed the door.

**Chorus**

# Mrs. White Had a Fright

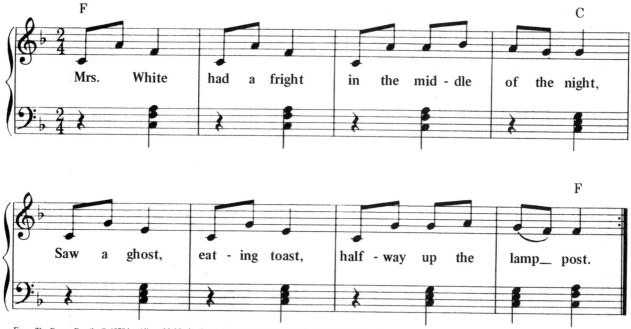

From *The Funny Family* © 1978 by Alison McMorland, reprinted by permission of Ward Lock Educational.

Mrs. White had a fright
In the middle of the night.
Saw a ghost, eating toast,
Halfway up the lamp post.

Mrs. Brown went to town
Just to buy an old nightgown.
Couldn't find one; bought a sweater,
Put it on and felt much better.

Mrs. Grimm, very trim,
Loved to dive and loved to swim.
Hit her head on the riverbed,
Never got up cause she died dead.

Mr. Sam, silly man,
Drank his tea from a frying pan,
Stirred his soup with a donkey's tail,
Scratched his belly with his big toenail.

Roy, Roy, dirty boy,
Cleaned his ears with a rubber toy,
Combed his hair with the leg of a chair,
Brushed his teeth with a polar bear.

Mrs. Mott used a pot
To cook her snails (or did she not?).
When she was through, she added glue,
And stirred with her finger till it turned
        blue.

Mrs. Spink wore her mink
To wash the dishes in the sink.
And as soon as she was able,
Did the laundry in her sable.

Mrs. Bloom took her broom
To clean up the living room.
Saw some dust upon the floor,
Left it there forevermore.

Mr. Starr drove his car
Not too near and not too far.
Got a flat, grabbed his hat,
Walked away and said, "That's that!"

Betty Bean, dressed in green,
Never smiled—she was too mean.
Liked to bite, scream and fight,
Kicked her brother, out of spite!

# It Ain't Gonna Rain No More

**Chorus**
Oh, it ain't gonna rain no more, no more,
It ain't gonna rain no more.
So how the heck you gonna wash your
      neck,
If it ain't gonna rain no more.

# It Ain't Gonna Rain No More

Oh, a peanut sat on a railroad track.
Its heart was all a-flutter.
Along came the 5:05—
Oops—peanut butter.

### Chorus

Oh, a skinny old lady once took a bath.
She didn't tell a soul.
She forgot to put the stopper in,
And slid right down the hole.

### Chorus

A cow walked on the railroad track.
The train was coming fast.
The train got off the railroad track
To let the cow go past.

### Chorus

A boy stood on a burning deck.
His feet were full of blisters.
He tore his pants on a rusty nail,
And now he wears his sister's.

### Chorus

Oh, there ain't no bugs on me,
There ain't no bugs on me.
There may be bugs on some of you mugs,
But there ain't no bugs on me.

### Chorus

I woke up in the morning.
I glanced upon the wall.
The roaches and the bedbugs
Were having a game of ball.

The score was six to nothing.
The roaches were ahead.
A bedbug hit a home run
And knocked me out of bed.

### Chorus

Billy Sunday is a preacher.
His church is always full.
The neighbors come from miles around
To hear him shoot the bull.

### Chorus

Well, the monkey swings by the end of his
      tail,
And jumps from tree to tree.
There may be monkey in some of you guys,
But there ain't no monkey in me.

### Chorus

Oh, a man was standing by a sewer,
And by a sewer he died.
They took him to his funeral
And called it sewer-cide!

### Chorus

There ain't no flies on me,
There ain't no flies on me,
There may be flies on some of you guys,
But there ain't no flies on me!

# Threw It Out the Window

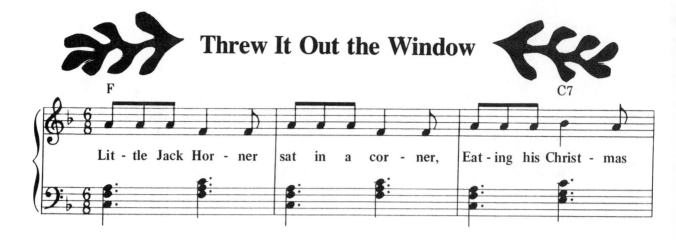

Lit - tle Jack Hor - ner sat in a cor - ner, Eat - ing his Christ - mas

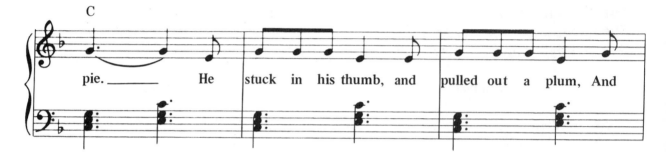

pie. _____ He stuck in his thumb, and pulled out a plum, And

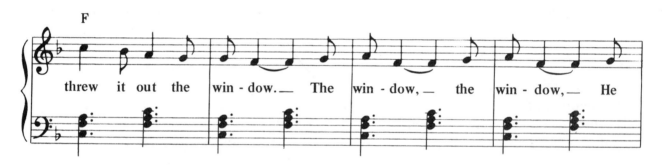

threw it out the win - dow. _ The win - dow, _ the win - dow, _ He

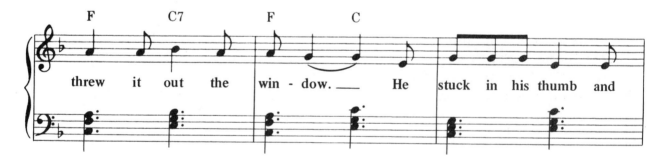

threw it out the win - dow. _ He stuck in his thumb and

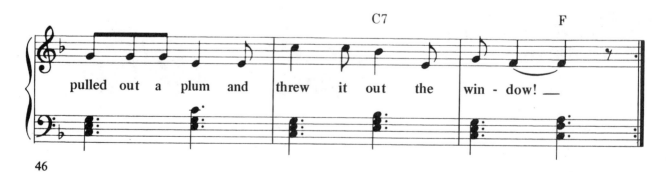

pulled out a plum and threw it out the win - dow! _

46

 # Threw It Out the Window

Little Jack Horner sat in a corner,
Eating his Christmas pie—
He stuck in his thumb, and pulled out a
plum,
And threw it out the window,
The window, the window,
He threw it out the window.
He stuck in his thumb and pulled out a
plum
And threw it out the window!

Little Miss Muffet, sat on a tuffet,
Eating her curds and whey—
Along came a spider, and sat down beside
her,
And threw it out the window,
The window, the window,
He threw it out the window.
Along came a spider and sat down beside
her
And threw it out the window!

Little Bo Peep has lost her sheep
And doesn't know where to find them—
Leave them alone and they'll come home
And we'll throw them out the window!
The window, the window,
We'll throw them out the window.
Leave them alone and they'll come home
And we'll throw them out the window!

Mary had a little lamb,
Little lamb, little lamb—
Mary had a little lamb
And threw it out the window,
The window, the window,
She threw it out the window.
Mary had a little lamb
And threw it out the window!

Old Mother Hubbard went to the cupboard
To find her poor dog a bone.
When she got there, the cupboard was
bare,
So she threw it out the window.
The window, the window,
She threw it out the window.
When she got there, the cupboard was
bare,
So she threw it out the window!

Georgie Peorgie, pudding and pie,
Kissed the girls and made them cry—
And when the boys began to play,
He threw them out the window.
The window, the window,
He threw them out the window.
And when the boys began to play,
He threw them out the window!

Jack and Jill went up the hill
To fetch a pail of water—
And Jack fell down and broke his crown
And threw it out the window.
The window, the window,
He threw it out the window.
And Jack fell down and broke his crown
And threw it out the window!

Little Boy Blue, come blow your horn,
The sheep's in the meadow, the cow's in
the corn.
Is that the way you mind your sheep?
We'll throw them out the window.
The window, the window,
We'll throw them out the window.
Is that the way you mind your sheep?
We'll throw them out the window!

# Fooba Wooba John

Saw a snake, bake a cake, Foo-ba woo-ba, foo-ba woo-ba,

Saw a snake, bake a cake, Foo-ba woo-ba John.

Saw a snake, bake a cake In the mid-dle of the lake,

Hey John, ho John, Foo-ba woo-ba John.

# Fooba Wooba John

Saw a snake, bake a cake,
Fooba wooba, fooba wooba,
Saw a snake, bake a cake,
Fooba wooba John.
Saw a snake, bake a cake
In the middle of the lake
Hey John, ho John,
Fooba wooba John.

Saw a seal, eat his meal,
Fooba wooba, fooba wooba,
Saw a seal, eat his meal,
Fooba wooba John.
Saw a seal, eat his meal,
While he made a business deal,
Hey John, ho John,
Fooba wooba John.

Saw a goose, letting loose,
Fooba wooba, fooba wooba,
Saw a goose, letting loose,
Fooba wooba John.
Saw a goose, letting loose
With her feathers all chartreuse,
Hey John, ho John,
Fooba wooba John.

Saw a bus, filled with us,
Fooba wooba, fooba wooba,
Saw a bus, filled with us,
Fooba wooba John.
Saw a bus, filled with us,
Making a terrific fuss,
Hey John, ho John,
Fooba wooba John.

Saw a bird, how absurd,
Fooba wooba, fooba wooba,
Saw a bird, how absurd,
Fooba wooba John.
Saw a bird, how absurd,
Eating all his whey and curd,
Hey John, ho John,
Fooba wooba John.

Saw a mule, on a stool,
Fooba wooba, fooba wooba,
Saw a mule, on a stool,
Fooba wooba John.
Saw a mule, on a stool,
Play a winning game of pool,
Hey John, ho John,
Fooba wooba John.

49

# Fooba Wooba John (continued)

Saw a broom, sweep the room,
Fooba wooba, fooba wooba,
Saw a broom, sweep the room,
Fooba wooba John.
Saw a broom, sweep the room,
Bang the walls with a big boom boom,
Hey John, ho John,
Fooba wooba John.

Saw a mop, jump and hop,
Fooba wooba, fooba wooba,
Saw a mop, jump and hop,
Fooba wooba John.
Saw a mop, jump and hop,
As it cleaned the counter top,
Hey John, ho John,
Fooba wooba John.

Saw an ant, tried but can't,
Fooba wooba, fooba wooba,
Saw an ant, tried but can't,
Fooba wooba John.
Saw an ant, tried but can't
Eat a prickly cactus plant,
Hey John, ho John,
Fooba wooba John.

Saw a chair, in the air,
Fooba wooba, fooba wooba,
Saw a chair, in the air,
Fooba wooba John.
Saw a chair, in the air,
Want to fly, but didn't dare,
Hey John, ho John,
Fooba wooba John.

Saw a hen, count to ten,
Fooba wooba, fooba wooba,
Saw a hen, count to ten,
Fooba wooba John.
Saw a hen, count to ten,
Then she counted down again,
Hey John, ho John,
Fooba wooba John.

Saw a bee, on one knee,
Fooba wooba, fooba wooba,
Saw a bee, on one knee,
Fooba wooba John.
Saw a bee, on one knee,
Kneeling down to talk to me,
Hey John, ho John,
Fooba wooba John.

# Up in the Air, Junior Bird Man

Up in the air, Jun - ior Bird Man, ___ up in the

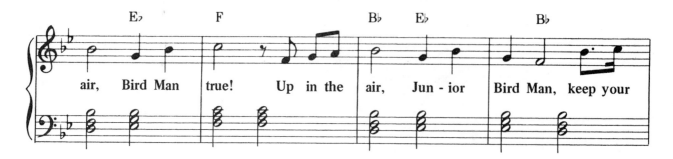

air, Bird Man true! Up in the air, Jun - ior Bird Man, keep your

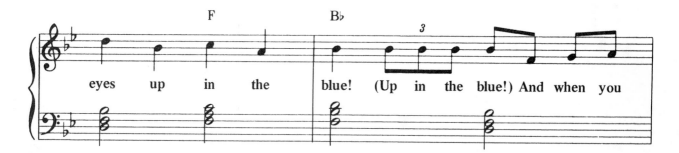

eyes up in the blue! (Up in the blue!) And when you

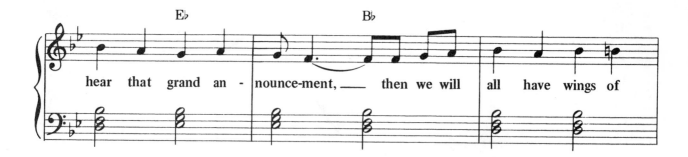

hear that grand an - nounce-ment, ___ then we will all have wings of

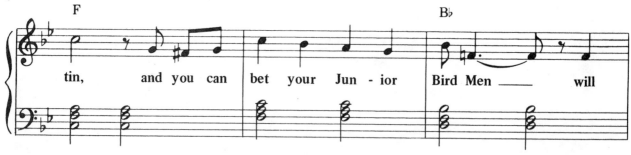

tin, and you can bet your Jun - ior Bird Men ___ will

# Up in the Air, Junior Bird Man

send their box-tops in! It takes just four box-tops. And six bot-tle bot-toms!

Up in the air, Junior Bird Man,
Up in the air, Bird Man true!
Up in the air, Junior Bird Man,
Keep your eyes up in the blue!
(Up in the blue!)

And when you hear that grand announcement,
Then we will all have wings of tin,
And you can bet your Junior Bird Men
    will send their boxtops in!

It takes just four---------
Boxtops

And six---------
Bottle bottoms!

(*spoken*) Whoooooooooossssssshhhhhhhh!

# John Brown's Baby

This is a jigsaw song. Each time you sing it, you leave out another part until barely a shell is left. Then put the pieces back and sing the song again. It's like breaking apart and rebuilding your own jigsaw puzzle.

First, you sing the song without motions. The second time leave out the word "baby" in every line. Make believe you're rocking a baby in your arms instead. The third time, in addition to "baby," leave out "cold" in each line. Sneeze or cough and shake your head, instead. The fourth time, besides "baby" and "cold," tap your chest with a loud thud instead of saying "chest." The fifth time you leave out "rubbed it in" and rub your chest in a circle instead. Finally, for "camphorated oil," hold your nose and make a face (it smells bad).

From *Musical Games for Children of All Ages*
© 1976 by Esther L. Nelson, reprinted by permission of Sterling Publishing Co., Inc.

# John Brown's Baby

John Brown's _____ had a _____ upon his _____,
(rock)       (cough)           (tap)

John Brown's _____ had a _____ upon his _____,
(rock)       (cough)           (tap)

John Brown's _____ had a _____ upon his _____,
(rock)       (cough)           (tap)

And they _____ with _____.
(rub it in)        (hold nose)

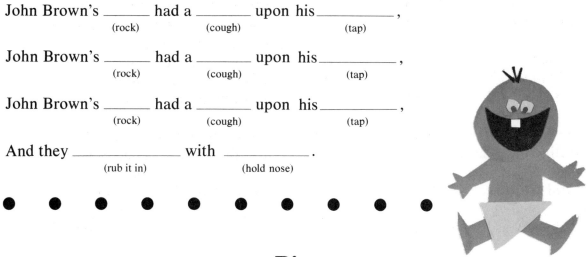

# Bingo

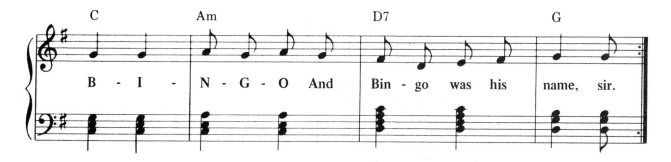

# Bingo (continued)

There was a farmer had a dog,
And Bingo was his name, sir.
B-I-N-G-O,
B-I-N-G-O,
B-I-N-G-O,
And Bingo was his name, sir.

There was a farmer had a dog,
And Bingo was his name, sir.
(*Clap*) I-N-G-O,
(*Clap*) I-N-G-O,
(*Clap*) I-N-G-O
And Bingo was his name, sir.

There was a farmer had a dog,
And Bingo was his name, sir.
(*Clap, clap*) N-G-O,
(*Clap, clap*) N-G-O,
(*Clap, clap*) N-G-O
And Bingo was his name, sir.

There was a farmer had a dog,
And Bingo was his name, sir.
(*Clap, clap, clap*) G-O,
(*Clap, clap, clap*) G-O,
(*Clap, clap, clap*) G-O
And Bingo was his name, sir.

There was a farmer had a dog,
And Bingo was his name, sir.
(*Clap, clap, clap, clap*) O,
(*Clap, clap, clap, clap*) O,
(*Clap, clap, clap, clap*) O
And Bingo was his name, sir.

There was a farmer had a dog,
And Bingo was his name, sir.
(*Clap, clap, clap, clap, clap*)
(*Clap, clap, clap, clap, clap*)
(*Clap, clap, clap, clap, clap*)
And Bingo was his name, sir.

The farmer's dog's at our back door,
Beggin' for a bone, sir.
B-I-N-G-O,
B-I-N-G-O,
B-I-N-G-O
And Bingo was his name, sir.

● ● ● ● ● ● ● ● ●

# Oh, Chester!

Oh, Chester, have you heard about
  Harry—
Just got back from the army,
I hear he knows how to wear his clothes—
Hip hip hooray for the army!

# Oh, Chester!

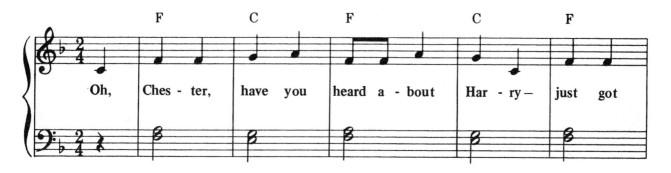

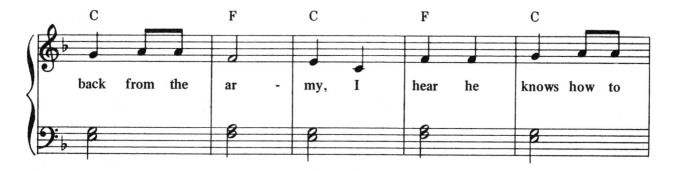

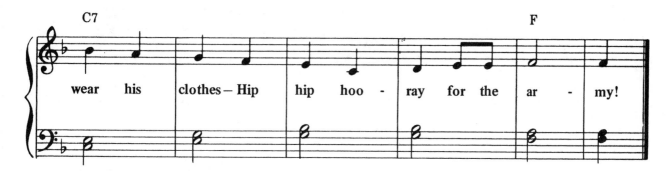

This is another jigsaw song. Sing it the same way as "John Brown's Baby."

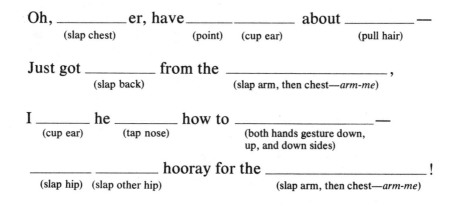

Oh, _____ er, have_____ _____ about _____ —
     (slap chest)          (point)  (cup ear)       (pull hair)

Just got _____ from the _____ ,
      (slap back)       (slap arm, then chest—*arm-me*)

I _____ he _____ how to _____ —
  (cup ear)     (tap nose)    (both hands gesture down,
                       up, and down sides)

_____ _____ hooray for the _____ !
(slap hip)  (slap other hip)        (slap arm, then chest—*arm-me*)

# A Fly Walked into a Grocery Store

A fly walked in-to a gro-cery store, A-

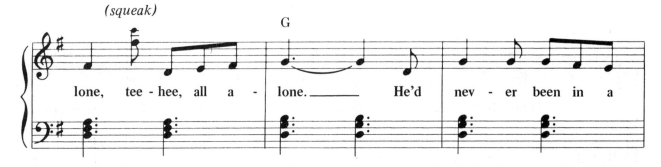

lone, tee-hee, all a-lone._____ He'd nev-er been in a

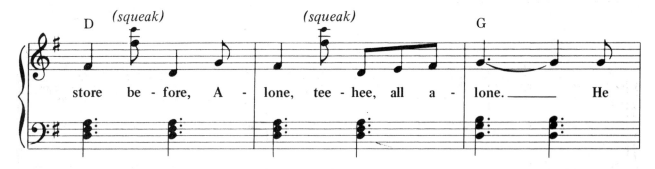

store be-fore, A-lone, tee-hee, all a-lone._____ He

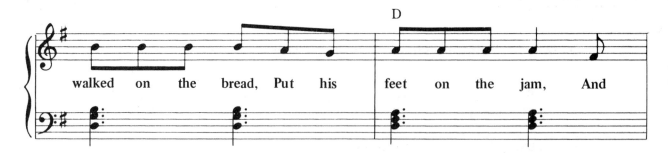

walked on the bread, Put his feet on the jam, And

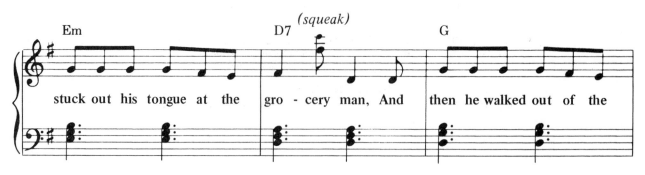

stuck out his tongue at the gro-cery man, And then he walked out of the

# A Fly Walked into a Grocery Store

*(squeak)*   *(squeak)*

store a - gain, A - lone, tee - hee, all a - lone._____

A fly walked into a grocery store—
Alone, tee-hee, all alone.

He'd never been in a store before—
Alone, tee-hee, all alone.

He walked on the bread,
Put his feet on the jam,
And stuck out his tongue at the grocery
    man,
And then he walked out of the store
    again—
Alone, tee-hee,
All alone.

# I'm Being Eaten by a Boa Constrictor

I'm be - ing eat - en by a bo - a con - strict - or!

I'm being eaten by a boa constrictor—
*(spoken)* Oh no, he's got my toe!
    Oh gee, he's got my knee!
    Oh my, he's got my thigh!
    Oh yip, he's got my hip!
    Make haste, he's got my waist!
    Be calm, he's got my arm!

That's grand, he's got my hand!
That bum, he's got my thumb!
Oh yes, he's got my chest!
Oh heck, he's got my neck!
Hey, Ted, he's got my head!
*(strangling)* Hemahonahoomangrahg . . . .

# The Hearse Song

Did you ev - er think, When the hearse goes by, That some day you are gon - na die?

*1st ending* D7

*2nd ending* D7 G

make out of you!

Did you ever think,
When the hearse goes by,
That some day you
Are gonna die?

The graveyard is
A lonely place.
They lay you down
And throw dirt in your face.

Everything's fine
For about a week,
Until the coffin
Begins to leak.

The worms crawl in,
The worms crawl out,
They crawl in through your stomach
And out of your mouth.

Your eyes drop out
And your teeth fall in,
And the worms crawl over
Your mouth and chin.

They bring their friends,
And relatives, too,
And boy! What a mess they can
Make out of you!

# Ghost Song

The | wom-an stood at the | old church door. | WHOO...WHOO...
YAAAAAAH!

The woman stood at the old church door.
    WHOO . . . WHOO . . .
    YAAAAAAH!

And she had not been there before.
    WHOO . . . WHOO . . .
    YAAAAAAH!

Oh, six long corpses were carried in.
    WHOO . . . WHOO . . .
    YAAAAAAH!

So very long and very thin.
    WHOO . . . WHOO . . .
    YAAAAAAH!

The woman to the corpses said,
    WHOO . . . WHOO . . .
    YAAAAAAH!

"Will I be thus when I am dead?"

(*Here, instead of the usual refrain,
SCREAM!*)

# Old MacTavish

From *Holiday Singing and Dancing Games*
© 1980 by Esther L. Nelson, reprinted by permission of Sterling Publishing Co., Inc.

Old MacTavish is dead, and his brother
don't know it.
His brother is dead and MacTavish don't
know it.
They're both of them dead, and they're in
the same bed—
So neither one knows that the other is
dead!

# SILLIER AND SILLIER

# This Old Man

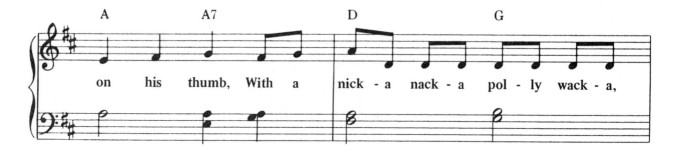

This old man, he plays one,
He plays nickanacka on his thumb,
With a nickanacka pollywacka, give a dog a bone,
This old man came rolling home.

This old man, he plays two,
He plays nickanacka on his shoe,
With a nickanacka pollywacka, give a dog a bone,
This old man came rolling home.

This old man, he plays three,
He plays nickanacka on his knee,
With a nickanacka pollywacka, give a dog a bone,
This old man came rolling home.

# This Old Man

This old man, he plays four,
He plays nickanacka on the floor,
With a nickanacka pollywacka, give a dog a bone,
This old man came rolling home.

This old man, he plays five,
He plays nickanacka on his side,
With a nickanacka pollywacka, give a dog a bone,
This old man came rolling home.

This old man, he plays six,
He plays nickanacka on his sticks,
With a nickanacka pollywacka, give a dog a bone,
This old man came rolling home.

This old man, he plays seven,
He plays nickanacka up in heaven,
With a nickanacka pollywacka, give a dog a bone,
This old man came rolling home.

This old man, he plays eight,
He plays nickanacka on the gate,
With a nickanacka pollywacka, give a dog a bone,
This old man came rolling home.

This old man, he plays nine,
He plays nickanacka all the time,
With a nickanacka pollywacka, give a dog a bone,
This old man came rolling home.

This old man, he plays ten,
He plays nickanacka over again,
With a nickanacka pollywacka, give a dog a bone,
This old man came rolling home.

# Bring Back My Neighbors to Me

One night as I lay on my pil - low, ___ One

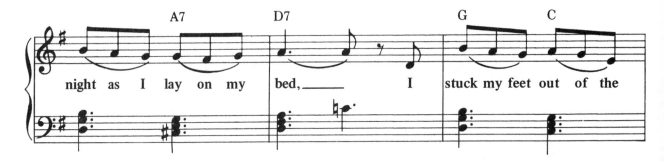

night as I lay on my bed, ___ I stuck my feet out of the

win - dow, ___ Next morn - ing my neigh - bors were dead.

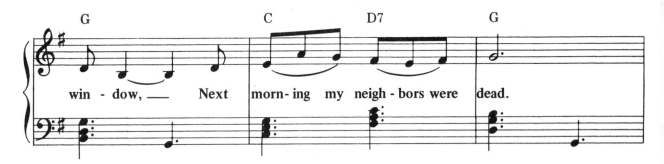

Chorus

Bring back, bring back, Oh bring back my neigh-bors to me, to me.

Bring back, bring back, Oh, bring back my neigh-bors to me.

# Bring Back My Neighbors to Me

One night as I lay on my pillow,
One night as I lay on my bed,
I stuck my feet out of the window,
Next morning my neighbors were dead.

One day as I sat in my rocker,
One day as I sat very still,
A firecracker killed off my neighbors,
And made me exceedingly ill.

### Chorus

Bring back, bring back,
Oh, bring back my neighbors to me, to me.
Bring back, bring back,
Oh, bring back my neighbors to me.

### Chorus

My neighbors looked into the gas tank,
But nothing inside could they see.
They lighted a match to assist them,
Oh, bring back my neighbors to me!

## To the same tune:

# The Wrong End

Oh, rabbits have bright, shiny noses,
I'm telling you this as a friend.
The reason their noses are shiny:
The powder puff's on the wrong end.

Wrong end—wrong end—
The powder puff's on the wrong end—
Wrong end—

Wrong end—wrong end—
The powder puff's on the wrong end!

# I Was Only Only Foolin'

I wear my silk pa-ja-mas In the sum-mer when it's

hot, And I wear my flan-nel night-ie in the win-ter when it's

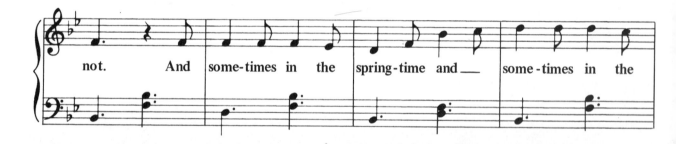

not. And some-times in the spring-time and ___ some-times in the

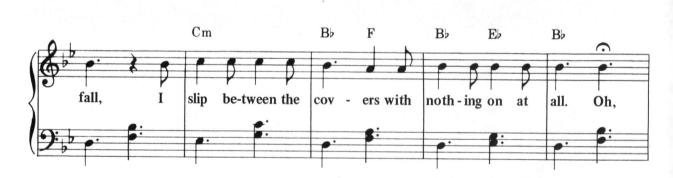

fall, I slip be-tween the cov-ers with noth-ing on at all. Oh,

**Chorus**

I ___ was on-ly, on-ly fool-in', I ___ was

# I Was Only Only Foolin'

I wear my silk pajamas
In the summer when it's hot,
And I wear my flannel nightie
In the winter when it's not.

And sometimes in the springtime
And sometimes in the fall,
I slip between the covers with
Nothing on at all.

### Chorus
Oh, I was only only foolin',
I was only only foolin',
I was only only foolin'
About the springtime and the fall.

I blast off in my rocket ship to visit on the
    moon,
And when I drive my submarine, I sing a
    silly tune,
And when I use my parachute, I float so
    gently down
And land with a bump in my own home
    town.

### Chorus
I was only foolin',
I was only foolin',
I was only foolin'
About my own home town.

# Greasy Grimy Gopher Guts

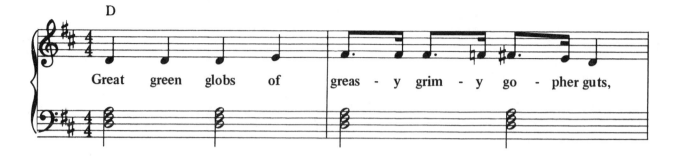

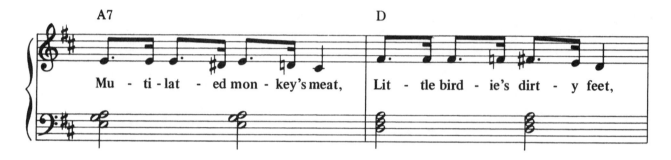

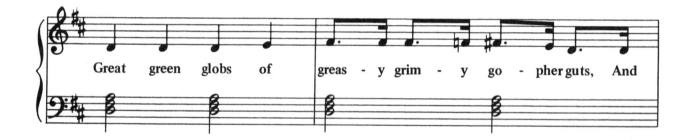

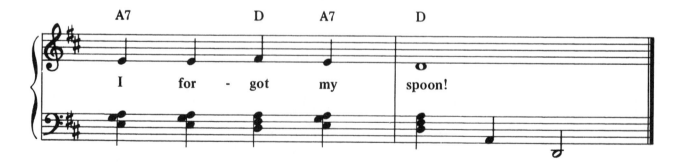

Great green globs of greasy grimy gopher
guts,
Mutilated monkey's meat,
Little birdie's dirty feet,
Great green globs of greasy grimy gopher
guts,
And I forgot my spoon!

# Everybody Hates Us

# Today is Monday

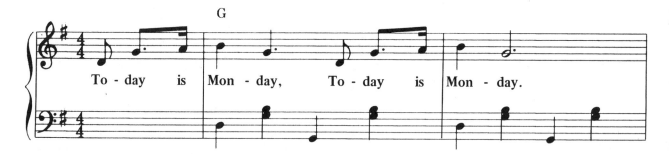

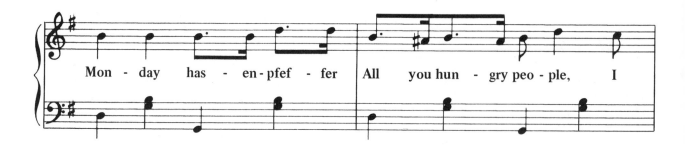

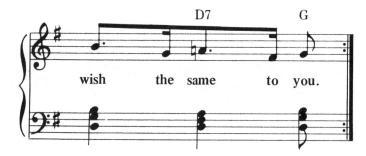

Today is Monday,
Today is Monday.
Monday hasenpfeffer,
All you hungry people,
I wish the same to you.

Today is Tuesday,
Today is Tuesday.
Tuesday pizza—Monday, hasenpfeffer,
All you hungry people,
I wish the same to you.

# Today is Monday

Today is Wednesday,
Today is Wednesday.
Wednesday soooooooooop —Tuesday
       pizza—Monday hasenpfeffer,
All you hungry people,
I wish the same to you.

Today is Thursday,
Today is Thursday.
Thursday shish-ka-bob—Wednesday
       soooooooop—Tuesday pizza—
       Monday hasenpfeffer,
All you hungry people,
I wish the same to you.

Today is Friday,
Today is Friday.
Friday felafel—Thursday shish-ka-bob—
      Wednesday soooooooop—Tuesday
      pizza—Monday hasenpfeffer,
All you hungry people,
I wish the same to you.

Today is Saturday
Today is Saturday
Saturday payday—Friday felafel—
      Thursday shish-ka-bob—
      Wednesday soooooooop—Tuesday
      pizza—Monday hasenpfeffer,
All you hungry people,
I wish the same to you.

# Chumbara . . . Chubearski . . . Feedoli

Chumbara, chumbara,
Chumbara, chumbara,
Chumbara, chumbara,
Chum, chum, chum, chum, chum,
Chum, chum, chum,

Chumbara, chumbara,
Chumbara, chumbara,
Chumbara, chumbara,
Chum, chum, chum!

# Chumbara . . . Chubearski . . . Feedoli

Chubearski, chubearski,
Chubearski, chubearski,
Chubearski, chubearski,
Chu, chu, chu, chu, chu,
Chu, chu, chu,
Chubearski, chubearski,
Chubearski, chubearski,
Chubearski, chubearski,
Chu, chu, chu!

Feedoli, feedoli,
Feedoli, feedoli,
Feedoli, feedoli,
Fee, fee, fee, fee, fee,
Fee, fee, fee,
Feedoli, feedoli,
Feedoli, feedoli,
Feedoli, feedoli,
Fee, fee, fee!

## Animal Fair

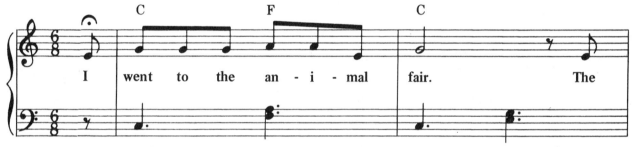

I went to the an - i - mal fair. The

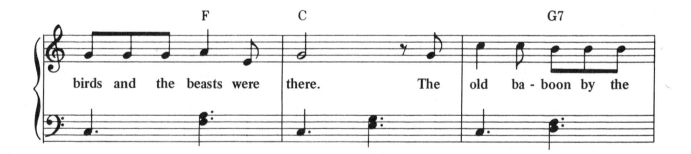

birds and the beasts were there. The old ba - boon by the

light of the moon was comb - ing his au - burn hair. The

# Animal Fair (continued)

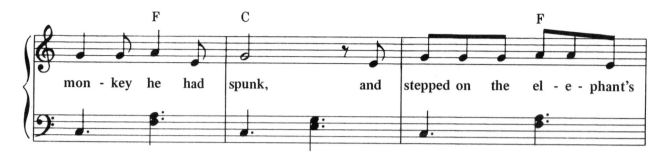

mon - key he had spunk, and stepped on the el - e - phant's

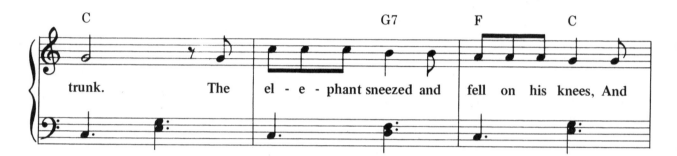

trunk. The el - e - phant sneezed and fell on his knees, And

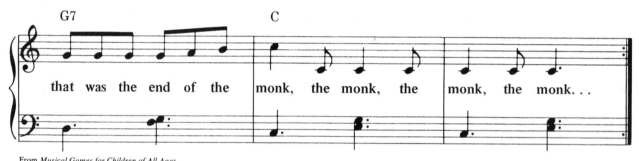

that was the end of the monk, the monk, the monk, the monk...

I went to the animal fair.
The birds and the beasts were there.
The old baboon by the light of the moon
Was combing his auburn hair.

The monkey he had spunk,
And stepped on the elephant's trunk.
The elephant sneezed and fell on his knees
And that was the end of the monk, the
    monk, the monk, the monk . . .

## I Like To Eat (or The Vowel Song)

I like to eat
    (I like to eat)
8 apples and bananas.
I like to eat
    (I like to eat)
8 apples and bananas.

Aye lake tay ate
    (Aye lake tay ate)
8 aypples aynd baynaynays.
Aye lake tay ate
    (Aye lake tay ate)
8 aypples aynd baynaynays.

# I Like To Eat (or The Vowel Song, continued)

Ee leek tee eat
    (Ee leek tee eat)
Eet eepples eend beeneenees.
Ee leek tee eat
    (Ee leek tee eat)
Eet eepples eend beeneenees.

Oh loke toe ote
    (Oh loke toe ote)
Ote ohpples ohnd bohnohnohs.
Oh loke toe ote
    (Oh loke toe ote)
Ote ohpples ohnd bohnohnohs.

I like ty ite
    (I like ty ite)
Ite iples iynd byenyenyes.
I like ty ite
    (I like ty ite)
Ite iples iynd byenyenyes.

Ooh loove too oot
    (Ooh loove too oot)
Oot oopples oond boonoonoos.
Ooh luve too oot
    (Ooh luve too oot)
Oot oopples oond boonoonoos.

# Young Folks, Old Folks

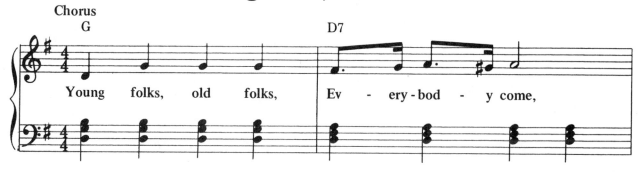

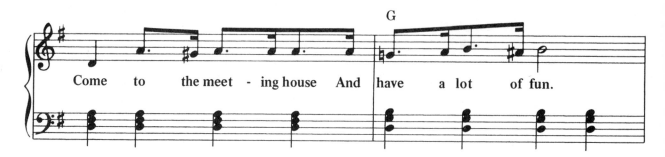

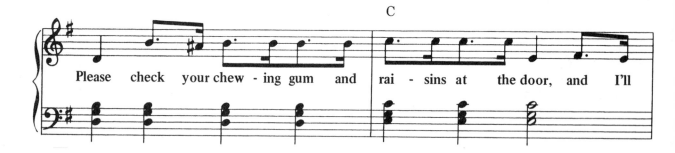

**Chorus**

Young folks, old folks,
Everybody come.
Come to the meeting house
And have a lot of fun.

Please check your chewing gum
And raisins at the door,
And I'll tell you Bible stories
That you never heard before.

# Young Folks, Old Folks

Salomey was a dancer and
She danced the hoochy kooch.
She danced before the King
And he liked it very mooch.

The Queen said, "Salomey,
We'll have no scandal here,"
Soo "Whoops," said Salomey,
And she kicked the chandelier.

# Young Folks, Old Folks (continued)

**Chorus**

God made Satan
And Satan made sin.
God made a hot place
To put Satan in.

Satan didn't like it,
So he said he wouldn't stay.
He's been acting like the devil
Ever since that sorry day.

**Chorus**

The world was built in six days,
And finished on the seventh.
According to the contract,
It should have been the eleventh.

The masons they got tired,
And the carpenters wouldn't work,
So the only thing that they could do
Was fill it up with dirt.

**Chorus**

Adam was the first man,
And Eve she was his spouse.
They got themselves together,
And they started keeping house.

One day they had a son—
And Abel was his name,
And everything went fine until
They started raising Cain.

**Chorus**

Adam was a good man.
Children he had seven.
Thought he'd hire a donkey cart
And take them all to heaven.

Strange to say, he lost the way,
Although he knew it well,
And  over went the donkey cart,
And sent them all to hell.

**Chorus**

Jonah was a sailor,
He set out for a sail.
He took a first-class passage
On a transatlantic whale.

He didn't like his quarters,
Although they were the best,
So Jonah pushed the button
And the whaley did the rest.

**Chorus**

David was a wise guy,
A wiry little cuss.
Along came Goliath,
A-looking for a fuss.

David fetched a stone,
And conked him on the dome,
And Goliath heard the birdies singing,
"Home sweet home."

**Chorus**

Sampson was a strong man,
You bet he was no fool.
He killed ten thousand Philistines
With the jawbone of a mule.

A woman named Delilah,
She cut his hair real thin,
And when he came to afterwards,
The coppers pulled him in.

**Chorus**

# SONGS THAT WON'T END

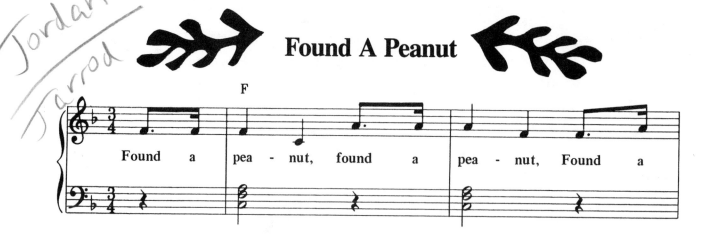

# Found A Peanut

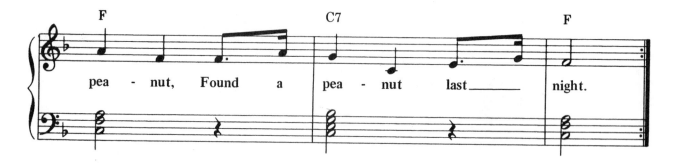

Found a peanut, found a peanut,
Found a peanut last night.
Last night I found a peanut,
Found a peanut last night.

Broke it open, broke it open,
Broke it open last night.
Last night I broke it open,
Broke it open last night.

Found it rotten, found it rotten,
Found it rotten last night.
Last night I found it rotten
Found it rotten last night.

Ate it anyway, ate it anyway,
Ate it anyway last night.
Last night I ate it anyway,
Ate it anyway, last night.

Got a tummyache, got a tummyache,
Got a tummyache last night.
Last night I got a tummyache,
Got a tummyache last night.

Called the doctor, called the doctor,
Called the doctor last night.
Last night I called the doctor,
Called the doctor last night.

# Found A Peanut

Appendicitis, appendicitis,
Appendicitis last night.
Last night appendicitis,
Appendicitis last night.

An operation, an operation,
An operation last night.
Last night an operation,
An operation last night.

Died anyway, died anyway,
Died anyway last night.
Last night I died anyway,
Died anyway last night.

Went to heaven, went to heaven,
Went to heaven last night.
Last night I went to heaven,
Went to heaven last night.

Wouldn't take me, wouldn't take me,
Wouldn't take me last night.
Last night they wouldn't take me,
Wouldn't take me last night.

Went the other way, went the other way,
Went the other way last night.
Last night I went the other way,
Went the other way last night.

Found it all a dream, found it all a dream,
Found it all a dream last night.
Last night I found it all a dream,
Found it all a dream last night.

Found a peanut, found a peanut,
Found a peanut last night.
Last night I found a peanut,
Found a peanut last night.

  Lasagna (Round)

La - sa - gna, baked zi - ti,

pa - sta - fa - zoo - la, we love thee!

# Oh, I Went Into the Water

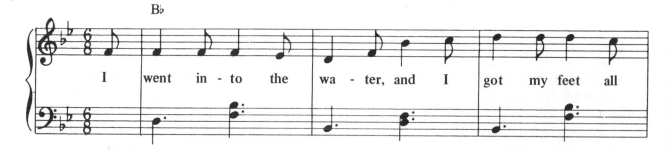

I went in-to the wa-ter, and I got my feet all

wet. I went in-to the wa-ter and I

got my feet all wet. I went in-to the

wa-ter, and I got my feet all wet, but I

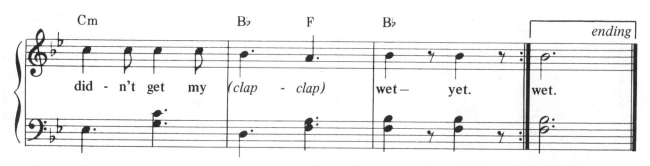

did-n't get my *(clap - clap)* wet— yet. | wet.

# Oh, I Went Into the Water

Oh, I went into the water,
And I got my feet all wet.
I went into the water,
And I got my feet all wet.
I went into the water,
And I got my feet all wet.
But I didn't get my (*clap, clap*) wet—yet.

Oh, I went into the water,
And I got my ankles wet.
I went into the water,
And I got my ankles wet.
I went into the water,
And I got my ankles wet.
But I didn't get my (*clap, clap*) wet—yet.

Oh, I went into the water,
And I got my legs all wet.
> (*and so on, up to
> your head*)

**Last stanza:**
Oh, I went into the water,
But I didn't get it wet.
I went into the water,
But I didn't get it wet.
I went into the water,
But I didn't get it wet.
I didn't get my camera wet.

# Goose Round

Why shouldn't my goose
Sing as well as thy goose,
When I paid for my goose
Twice as much as thou?

# A Bear Climbed Over the Mountain

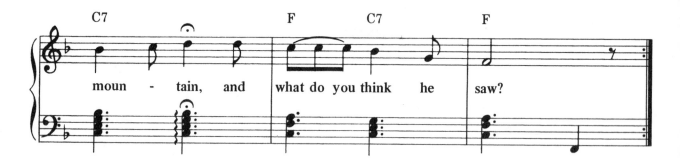

A bear climbed over the mountain,
A bear climbed over the mountain,
A bear climbed over the mountain,
And what do you think he saw?

He saw another mountain,
He saw another mountain,
He saw another mountain,
And what do you think he did?

He climbed the other mountain,
He climbed the other mountain,
He climbed the other mountain,
And what do you think he saw?

He saw another mountain,
He saw another mountain,
He saw another mountain,
And what do you think he did?

He climbed the other mountain,
He climbed the other mountain,
He climbed the other mountain,
And what do you think he saw?

*and so on . . .*
*and so on . . .*
*and so on . . .*

# Michael Finnegan

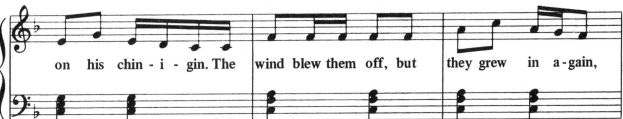

I know a man named Michael Finnegan.
He had whiskers on his chin-igin.
The wind blew them off, but they grew in
    again,
Poor old Michael Finnegan (begin again)—

I know a man named Michael Finnegan.
He went fishing with a pin-agin,
Caught a fish and dropped it in-agin,
Poor old Michael Finnegan (begin again)—

I know a man named Michael Finnegan.
Climbed a tree and barked his shin-agin,
Took off several yards of skin-igin,
Poor old Michael Finnegan (begin again)—

I know a man named Michael Finnegan.
He kicked up an awful din-igin,
Because they said he could not sing-igin,
Poor old Michael Finnegan (begin again)—

I know a man named Michael Finnegan.
He got fat and then got thin again,
Then he died and had to begin again,
Poor old Michael Finnegan (begin again)—

# Five Chartreuse Buzzards

Five chartreuse buzzards,
Five chartreuse buzzards,
Sitting on a fence,
Sitting on a fence,
    *(spoken:)*    Ooooooh, look.
    *(pointing:)*    One has flown aye-way.
                  Isn't that aye shame.

Four chartreuse buzzards,
Four chartreuse buzzards,
Sitting on a fence,
Sitting on a fence,
    *(spoken:)*    Ooooooh, look.
    *(pointing:)*    One has flown aye-way.
                  Isn't that aye shame.

Three chartreuse buzzards,
Three chartreuse buzzards,
Sitting on a fence,
Sitting on a fence,
    *(spoken:)*    Ooooooh, look.
    *(pointing:)*    One has flown aye-way.
                  Isn't that aye shame.

Two chartreuse buzzards,
Two chartreuse buzzards,
Sitting on a fence,
Sitting on a fence.
    *(spoken:)*    Ooooooh, look.
    *(pointing:)*    One has flown aye-way.
                  Isn't that
                      aaaaaaa-shame.

One chartreuse buzzard,
One chartreuse buzzard,
Sitting on a fence,
Sitting on a fence,
    *(spoken:)*    Ooooooh, look.
    *(pointing:)*    One has flown
                  aaaaaaaaa-way.
                  Isn't that
                      aaaaaaaaaa-shame.

No chartreuse buzzards,
No chartreuse buzzards,
Sitting on a fence,
Sitting on a fence,

# Five Chartreuse Buzzards

(spoken:)     Ooooooh, look.
(pointing:)   One has
                reeeeeeee-turned.
              Let us reeeeeeee-joice.

One chartreuse buzzard,
One chartreuse buzzard,
Sitting on a fence,
Sitting on a fence,
     (spoken:)     Ooooooh, look.
     (pointing:)   One has
                   reeeeeee-turned.
                Let us reeeeeeee-joice.

Two chartreuse buzzards,
         (and so on!)

 # To Ope Their Trunks    (Round)

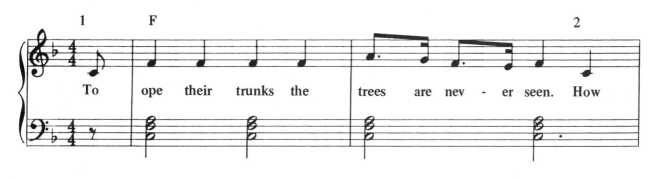

To ope their trunks the trees are nev - er seen. How

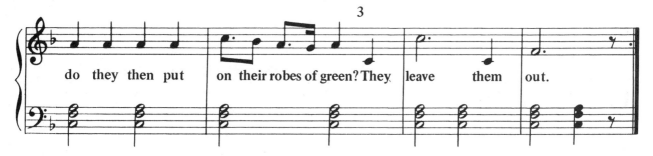

do they then put on their robes of green? They leave them out.

# There's a Hole in the Bottom of the Sea

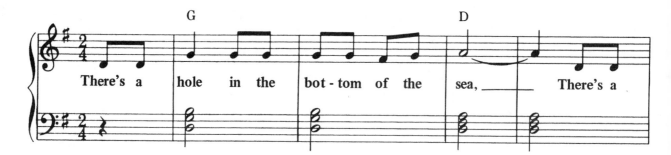

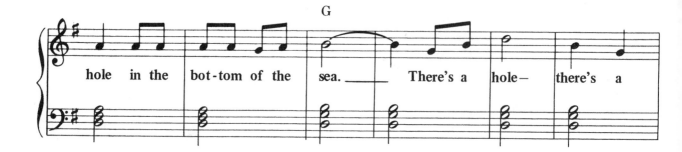

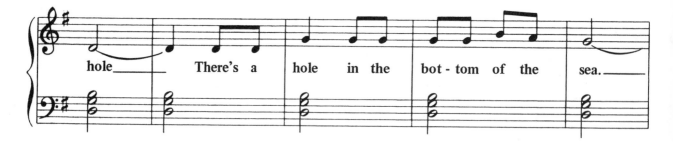

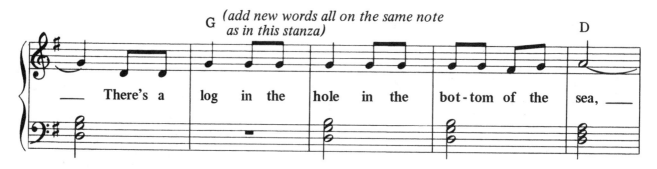

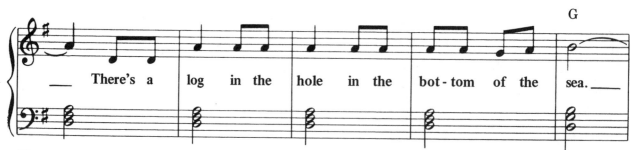

# There's a Hole in the Bottom of the Sea

There's a | log, | There's a | log, | There's a

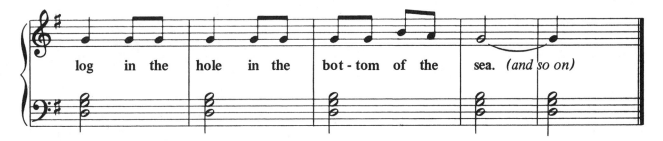

log | in the | hole | in the | bot - tom | of the | sea. *(and so on)*

There's a hole in the bottom of the sea.
There's a hole in the bottom of the sea.
There's a hole—there's a hole—
There's a hole in the bottom of the sea.

There's a log in the hole in the bottom of
the sea.
There's a log in the hole in the bottom of
the sea.
There's a log—there's a log—
There's a log in the hole in the bottom of
the sea.

There's a bump on the log in the hole in the
bottom of the sea.
There's a bump on the log in the hole in the
bottom of the sea.
There's a bump—there's a bump—
There's a bump on the log in the hole in the
bottom of the sea.

There's a frog on the bump on the log in the
hole in the bottom of the sea.
There's a frog on the bump on the log in the
hole in the bottom of the sea.
There's a frog—there's a frog—
There's a frog on the bump on the log in the
hole in the bottom of the sea.

There's a wart on the frog on the bump on
the log in the hole in the bottom of
the sea.
There's a wart on the frog on the bump on
the log in the hole in the bottom of
the sea.
There's a wart—there's a wart—
There's a wart on the frog on the bump on
the log in the hole in the bottom of
the sea.

# There's a Hole in the Bottom of the Sea (continued)

There's a hair on the wart on the frog on the
  bump on the log in the hole in the
  bottom of the sea.
There's a hair on the wart on the frog on the
  bump on the log in the hole in the
  bottom of the sea.
There's a hair—there's a hair—
There's a hair on the wart on the frog on the
  bump on the log in the hole in the
  bottom of the sea.

There's a fly on the hair on the wart on the
  frog on the bump on the log in the
  hole in the bottom of the sea.
There's a fly on the hair on the wart on the
  frog on the bump on the log in the
  hole in the bottom of the sea.

There's a fly—there's a fly—
There's a fly on the hair on the wart on the
  frog on the bump on the log in the
  hole in the bottom of the sea.

There's a speck on the fly on the hair on the
  wart on the frog on the bump on
  the log in the hole in the bottom of
  the sea.
There's a speck on the fly on the hair on the
  wart on the frog on the bump on
  the log in the hole in the bottom of
  the sea.
There's a speck—there's a speck—
There's a speck on the fly on the hair on the
  wart on the frog on the bump on
  the log in the hole in the bottom of
  the sea.

# On Mules We Find

On mules we find
2 legs behind
and 2 we find
before.

We stand behind
before we find
what the 2 behind
be for.

When we're behind
the 2 behind,
we find what they
be for.

So stand before
the 2 behind,
behind the 2
before!

# To the same tune:

# We're Here!

We're here because
We're here because
We're here because
We're here.

We're here because
We're here because
We're here because
We're here.

# On Mules We Find

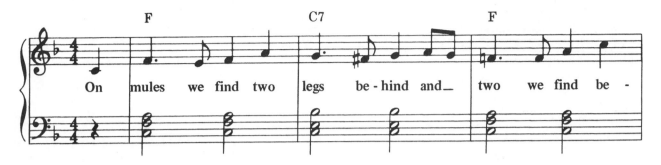

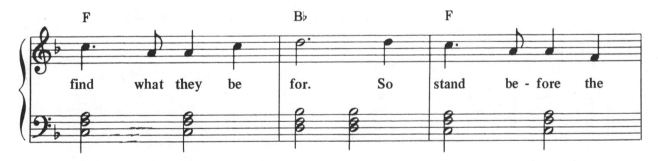

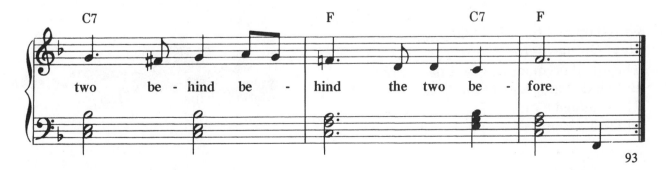

# Grasshoppers Three    (Round)

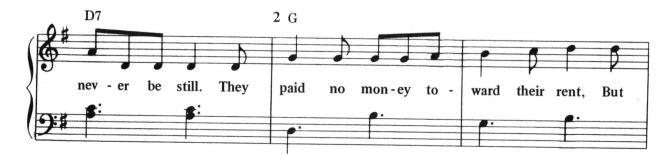

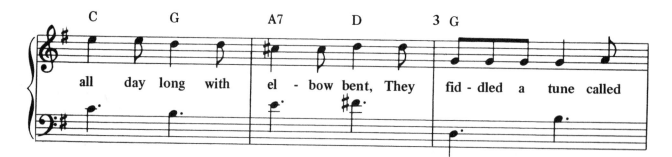

Grasshoppers three a-fiddling went,
Hey! Ho! never be still.
They paid no money toward their rent,
But all day long with elbow bent,
They fiddled a tune called ril-la-by, ril-la-by,
Fiddled a tune called ril-la-by rill.

# Roll Over

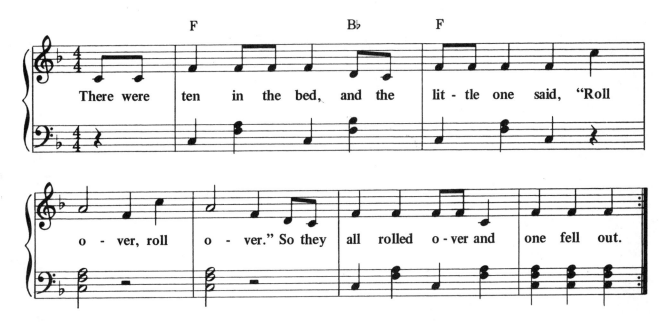

There were ten in the bed
And the little one said,
"Roll over, roll over."
So they all rolled over
And one fell out.

There were nine in the bed
And the little one said,
"Roll over, roll over."
So they all rolled over
And one fell out.

There were eight in the bed
And the little one said,
"Roll over, roll over."
So they all rolled over
And one fell out.

There were seven in the bed
And the little one said,
"Roll over, roll over."
So they all rolled over
And one fell out.

There were six in the bed
And the little one said,
"Roll over, roll over."
So they all rolled over
And one fell out.

There were five in the bed
And the little one said,
"Roll over, roll over."
So they all rolled over
And one fell out.

There were four in the bed
And the little one said,
"Roll over, roll over."
So they all rolled over
And one fell out.

There were three in the bed
And the little one said,
"Roll over, roll over."
So they all rolled over
And one fell out.

There were two in the bed
And the little one said,
"Roll over, roll over."
So they all rolled over
And one fell out.

There was one in the bed
And the little one said,
(spoken) "Goodnight."

95

# INDEX